ISLE OF WIGHT FOR BEGINNERS

From one holidaymaker to another

GLENDA SHEPHERD

Copyright © 2019 Glenda Shepherd
All rights reserved

The following places of interest and the restaurants that are included in this book have all been tried and tested by myself and my husband Phil.

All the photographs used are my own.

No part of this book may be reproduced in any written, electronic, recording, or photocopied form without written permission of the author. The exception would be in the case of brief quotations embodied in critical articles and reviews, and pages where permission is specifically granted by the author.

OTHER WORKS BY GLENDA SHEPHERD

My Journey Through Thyroid Cancer and Out the Other Side

Contents

Chapter 1: Getting There 1
Chapter 2: Alum Bay, Freshwater 5
Chapter 3: Arreton Manor, Arreton 10
Chapter 4: Carisbrooke Castle 12
Chapter 5: Godshill 17
Chapter 6: Isle of Wight Steam Railway 20
Chapter 7: Marc Tuckey's Ghost Walks 23
Chapter 8: St. Catherine's Lighthouse, Niton 25
Chapter 9: Osborne House 28
Chapter 10: Puckpool 32
Chapter 11: Quarr Abbey 35
Chapter 12: Robin Hill Park, Newport 37
Chapter 13: St. Helen's Beach 38
Chapter 14: St. Mildred's Church, Whippingham 41
Chapter 15: Sandown and Sandown Pier 44
Chapter 16: Shanklin Chine 46
Chapter 17: Steephill Cove 49
Chapter 18: The Isle of Wight Festival 51
Chapter 19: The Tennyson Trail, Freshwater 55
Chapter 20: Winkle Street 58
Chapter 21: Yar Estuary 60

Website Links Of Other Places To Visit 63

CHAPTER 1

GETTING THERE

The Isle of Wight is the perfect place to visit for young and old alike; there is something for everyone. From the moment you board the ferry, your holiday is underway (as of 2019 there are no toll bridges or tunnels linking the Isle of Wight with the mainland).

There are two ferry services to the Island – Red Funnel runs a high-speed service for foot passengers only from Southampton to West Cowes (takes about half an hour) and also there are car ferries from Southampton to East Cowes (takes about 1 hour).

Wightlink connects Lymington to Yarmouth, and also Portsmouth to Fishbourne (foot passengers and cars), and both take about 40 minutes. There is also a Fastcat passenger-only service from Portsmouth to Ryde, which takes about 20 -25 minutes. Phil and I have never had cause to use Red Funnel, as the holiday park where we have a caravan has a discount deal with Wightlink, and is also nearer to Fishbourne than Cowes.

Both services run every day and all year round. Of course during the peak summer season there will be extra ferries to cope with demand. Here are the addresses below:

Red Funnel **Southampton to East Cowes**
Terminal 1
Dock Gate 7 (Royal Pier)
Town Quay Road
Southampton, SO14 2AR

Red Funnel **Southampton to West Cowes**
Terminal 2
Town Quay
Southampton
SO14 2AQ

Wightlink **Lymington to Yarmouth**
Lymington ferry terminal
Undershore Road
Lymington
Hampshire
SO41 5SB

Wightlink Portsmouth to Fishbourne
Portsmouth ferry terminal
Gunwharf Road
Portsmouth
Hampshire
PO1 2LA

Below is one of the fleet of Wightlink car/passenger ferries (photo taken in July 2004). They also now have a £30m flagship, The Victoria of Wight, launched in 2018.

If you have a long wait for the ferry, walk through the iron gate on the right hand side near the old Portsmouth ticket building, and you can explore Gunwharf Quay and the Spinnaker Tower, or once on the Island you can book a hovercraft trip over to Southsea and explore the quay if you have a spare day.

GLENDA SHEPHERD

CHAPTER 2

ALUM BAY, FRESHWATER.
PO39 0JD

When I was a child, Alum Bay consisted of a stony beach below cliffs of coloured sands that was accessible by a steep chairlift or over 300 steps down if you didn't like heights. You could scrape off some of the colourful sands into a test tube as a souvenir of your visit. Also you could ride in a small boat out to the Needles rocks and lighthouse.

These days and 50 years on, much has changed. The chairlift and steps are still there, but a theme park with rides and a gift shop has emerged. You are not allowed to touch the coloured sands anymore, which are roped off as the cliffs have started to erode. However, you can buy a glass container in the gift shop and fill it up with sand that is provided there. There are also daily demonstrations of glass blowing near to the Marconi tea rooms.

The boat ride out to the Needles rocks and lighthouse is still available, once you have decided how to get down to the beach. The ride out is okay on a calm day, even for me! It takes about 40 minutes and there's a commentary and opportunities to take photos.

A brief walk away from the theme park and in a more natural setting is the Needles Battery, a Victorian military Battery now owned by the National Trust and built in the 1860s to guard the West end of the Solent.

Photo showing the chairlift leading down to Alum Bay, Freshwater.

View of the beach (mainly pebbles) and cliffs at Alum Bay from the chairlift.

On the boat out to the Needles rocks and lighthouse.

A short car ride away is the town of Freshwater, which is near to Afton Down where the famous 1970 Isle of Wight festival was held. The festival attracted over 600,000 people, and locals at the time had the delightful view of nude hippies bathing in the cold, choppy waters of Freshwater Bay! At Freshwater itself is an exhibition of photos from that festival at Dimbola Lodge, which was the home of the celebrated Victorian photographer Julia Margaret Cameron (Dimbola Lodge is not open on Mondays). There is a small tea room for refreshments next to Dimbola Lodge, or there is the excellent Delicia Café opposite the bay. You know when you've arrived at Dimbola, as there is a statue of Jimi Hendrix in the front garden!

Mr Hendrix and me at Dimbola Lodge.

ISLE OF WIGHT FOR BEGINNERS

CHAPTER 3

ARRETON MANOR, ARRETON
Main Road, Arreton, PO30 3AA

This manor house first sparked my interest because of its paranormal activity. There is a ghost of a young girl which has been seen around the corridors – Annabelle Leigh, who was murdered there in 1560 by her brother. Apparently chanting monks can sometimes be heard, and other strange occurrences are often experienced.

The house goes way back to 872 AD, and was left by King Alfred to his youngest son in his will. In the 12th century it became part of Quarr Abbey (the abbey is also mentioned in this book) and was used by the monks for over 400 years. The manor was re-built between 1595 and 1612 in the Jacobean style. There is a secret panel in the hallway, which leads out to the back of the house.

There are pretty gardens to stroll around, and if you're lucky the peacock will display his feathers. Opening hours are limited, and so it's best to check before you arrive.

CHAPTER 4

CARISBROOKE CASTLE
Castle Hill, Newport, PO30 1XY

I'm happy to announce that not much seems to change at Carisbrooke Castle. I have been there on several occasions over a period of about 30 years. Here I am up on the battlements in 2006, where we had also pushed our son in his buggy 20 years before. Lovely views from the top!

It's an interesting castle to explore. King Charles I was held there for 14 months until his execution in 1649 (he tried to escape but became stuck in a window). Here's some more views of the castle:

Queen Victoria's youngest daughter Beatrice lived there in the Governor's House from 1912 until her death in 1944. The house is shown below, and there is also Princess Beatrice's garden to look around.

There is a museum to visit, a chapel, and also a tearoom. Donkeys still work the old 16th century water wheel every day, bringing water up from a well 161 feet below. You can also visit the stables where the donkeys are kept.

Donkeys take it in turns every day to walk the wheel.

The chapel at Carisbrooke Castle.

Sometimes during the summer there are special events at the castle such as demonstrations of jousting. All in all, a good day out for the family.

CHAPTER 5

GODSHILL
Church Hill, Godshill, PO38 3HY

Godshill is situated towards the southeast of the Island between Newport and Ventnor, and so there is no beach. However, tourists flock to this small village (population about 1500) for its quaint shops, the picturesque thatched cottages, the model village, the restaurants and tea rooms, and to visit the medieval All Saints Church, high on the hill above. It's a bit of a climb!

Legend has it that originally the foundations for the church were laid in a flat, easily accessible site, but every morning the builders would return to find they had been transferred up the hill. Eventually they gave up and built the church on the hill.

Steps above leading to the medieval All Saints church.

You can imagine the slower pace of life in this quintessential English village back in Victorian times. Horses and carriages would meander along the narrow high street, which now has to cope with an influx of cars and coach tours in the busy summer season.

One of the many thatched tearooms/cottages in Godshill.

In the high street there are plenty of shops selling souvenirs and gifts. At one end of the village close to the large car park and public toilets there is a shopping complex, with shops selling clothes and gifts. Most people park here and walk along the narrow pavements (not a lot of room for 2 people to pass by!) to the tearooms, model village and church. There are many tearooms to choose from!

CHAPTER 6

ISLE OF WIGHT STEAM RAILWAY
Main Road, Havenstreet, PO33 4DS

Time to step back into the bygone era of steam locomotives at Havenstreet Station, the headquarters and depot of the Isle of Wight Steam Railway. There are several steam engines, the oldest one being built in 1864. The line operated as a public service from 1862 – 1966. Nowadays it's more a visitor attraction, with a somewhat reduced track running five and a half miles between Wootton and Smallbrook

When we visited it back in 2006 it reminded me of how train stations used to be in my childhood, with the uniformed guard, station waiting room and ticket office, the signal box, and the sidings with carriages. There is also a café there and a museum. The train ride is quite short, and it seemed strange to look out of the window and see steam coming from the engine!

It's quite educational for today's kids, who might be interested to see how their grandparents and great-grandparents travelled about, not to mention a boon for the steam engine enthusiasts.

CHAPTER 7

MARC TUCKEY'S GHOST WALKS

http://www.ghostisland.com/ghost_walks

https://www.facebook.com/iwghostexperience/

The Isle of Wight has more than its fair share of ghosts, and Marc Tuckey knows about most of them. These ghost walks are a lot of fun if you're not of a nervous disposition. We've been on about 5 walks over the years. Mr Tuckey dresses up in his Victorian garb and takes a group on a different walk every week, informing people of any relevant ghosts to the area. However, every now and then a 'gremlin' will jump out, so beware!

I think my favourite walk was the one around Ventor's Botanic Gardens. It was pitch dark in there, and very spooky. Gremlins appeared out of nowhere, wailing and screaming, while I tried to listen to the commentary which was quite interesting. Apparently the Botanic Gardens was built on the site of an old Victorian chest hospital, where TB patients were sent for the sea air. Ghosts of dead patients and nurses roam around the gardens, although thankfully I didn't see any at the time.

Other walks are around Shanklin and Carisbrooke (not in the castle though), and there was a walk we went on around St. Catherine's lighthouse at Niton, although I'm not sure that this one is still going on. A very enjoyable evening if you're interested in the paranormal (APRIL - OCTOBER).

Mr Tuckey with his top hat, lantern, and shedloads of ghost stories.

CHAPTER 8
ST. CATHERINE'S LIGHTHOUSE, NITON.
PO38 2NF

One of the previous stops on Mr Tuckey's ghost walk, St. Catherine's lighthouse is one of the oldest lighthouses in Great Britain, having been built in 1838 after the loss of The Clarendon ship near to where the lighthouse is situated (at the most southerly point on the Island). It also suffered damage from a bombing raid in 1943, which can still be seen when pointed out during a tour.

Opening hours vary, so anybody visiting the lighthouse will need to check first. However, it's very near to The Buddle Inn, a historic and pleasant pub in which to while away the time if you arrive too early.

There is a steep path opposite the pub which will eventually lead to the lighthouse, but you'll have to walk through a couple of fields first. We did this on a lovely summer day in 2009 as you can see from the photos, and there are marvellous views. There is NO VEHICLE ACCESS to the lighthouse, and so you'll need to put on your walking shoes!

There are quite a few steps up to the lantern, which has a range of 26 miles. It's well worth a visit if you're visiting the southern part of the Island and you have a reasonable level of fitness.

CHAPTER 9

OSBORNE HOUSE
York Avenue, East Cowes, PO32 6JX

Ah, dear Osborne House (the name will be changed to Royal Osborne soon). We've been there so many times that my husband reckons he knows it better than the late Queen Victoria herself!

Osborne House stands on 342 acres of grounds, and was bought by Prince Albert and Queen Victoria in 1845. After Prince Albert's death in 1861, Queen Victoria lived a hermit-like existence at Osborne for many years. Not only is the house still standing and in excellent condition, but there is also a Swiss Cottage a mile away on the grounds (accessible by walking or a courtesy bus) where Victoria and Albert's nine children learned to cook, grow their own vegetables, and keep house.

Osborne is fully furnished as it used to be back in the 1800s. I always find it fascinating to see plaster casts of the children's hands and feet in the nursery, and the bedroom where Queen Victoria died is especially atmospheric. Albert's photo is attached to his side of the bed…

This view above is taken from one of the upstairs windows at Osborne.

When you have looked around the house (photos are allowed), there are the extensive grounds to explore, including Queen Victoria's bathing machine down by the Swiss Cottage. There is also a café, a restaurant, a gift shop, and toilets. If you enjoy a horse and carriage ride, one is available which meanders around the grounds.

You'll need to spend a day here. Highly recommended.

CHAPTER 10

PUCKPOOL

Puckpool Hill, Seaview, PO34 5AR

This is one of my favourite places on the Island. The golden sands stretch all the way down to Ryde, and there's a lovely flat esplanade / walkway for cycling or walking. If you leave the car in Puckpool Park and walk towards the beach, there's a café on your right selling delicious food. Turn left (Appley Tower will be in front of you) and walk a quarter of a mile or so, and there is another café and a children's playground and toilets. Puckpool beach has lots of shade, for those (like me) who do not like to sit in the sun. Shade is missing on a lot of the Island's beaches, but Puckpool has large trees along the walkway which give great relief from the sun in the afternoons. The sands are always raked in the evenings, and it's a lovely beach for sure.

If you walk or cycle past the children's playground and café, there's a left turning up into Puckpool Park itself, or if you carry on there's a lake with pedalos, and Ryde swimming pool (pool usually opens at 3pm during school term time) and various rides and amusements along Ryde seafront. There's also a Laser Quest and Bowling alley. Further along at Ryde, there are many shops up a steep hill. You can park the car for the shops in St. Thomas' Street car park (**PO33 2DL**)

Below you can see Phil and I at Puckpool in 2012. I always love the colours of the sky, sea and sand there.

CHAPTER 11

QUARR ABBEY
QUARR ROAD, RYDE, PO33 4ES

Quarr Abbey, built in 1911/1912 is still a working monastery – you'll catch glimpses of the monks as they go about their daily business. This oasis of calm and peace lies not too far from the Fishbourne ferry terminal. Entry is free. You can sit in on a service, or just stroll through the beautiful grounds. There is a farm shop (selling produce grown in the grounds) and a tearoom. Donations are welcome!

CHAPTER 12

ROBIN HILL PARK, NEWPORT
PO30 2NU

Quite heavy on the legs for the uninitiated (it's all up hills and down dales), but there's quite often lots of interesting events happening there throughout the year. In the past we've been to the Festival of Light (based on 'Diwali') which is usually in October I think, and also Bestival, a music festival which has now been moved to a different location unfortunately. You can check what's on by following this link:

https://www.visitisleofwight.co.uk/whats-on

CHAPTER 13

ST. HELEN'S BEACH
PO33 1XZ (Baywatch Café postcode)

St. Helen's is a village on the East side of the Island, where all the houses and shops are centred around a delightful village green. During the summer there is a Sunday morning boot fair every week on the green, and if you're staying nearby, there is a Tesco supermarket at the end of the Beaper Shute (love that name!) and go-karting within a short walk of the supermarket. The beach is accessible by car, and there is The Baywatch Café serving teas, lunches and evening meals down on the sands (best to book for the evening), toilets, and also the chance to rent surfboards, kayaks and paddleboards during the summer months. There's also a path up through the trees to the next bays along.

Once a year in August at a low Spring tide, hundreds of people flock to the beach to take part in a walk to the Victorian fort, which can be seen from the beach. The whole shingle path can be seen at this particularly low tide, which gives you about an hour's window to get to the fort and back, maybe an hour and a half. It's about a 30 minute walk out to the fort, and be prepared for the walk being more strenuous than you think, due to the stones, slippery rocks and shifting shingle. When you get to the fort, it's good luck to climb up the short flight of steps and walk anti-clockwise around the ledge. On the organised walk the coastguard is in the background just in case, but on other occasions when the path is visible you're on your own!

You're quite likely to see Phil and I walking along the shoreline. Here are some photos of the beach, and also of the fort, which Phil and I have walked to:

CHAPTER 14

ST. MILDRED'S CHURCH, WHIPPINGHAM
BEATRICE AVENUE, EAST COWES, PO32 6LW

Situated close to Osborne House, Queen Victoria and her family often came here to attend services, weddings and funerals. Princess Beatrice, Queen Victoria's youngest daughter, is buried here in the church along with her husband Prince Henry of Battenberg. There are often exhibitions of royal memorabilia in the church, and there is also a small tea room but it is not always open.

Looking down the aisle at Whippingham Church. Princess Beatrice's tomb is down the end by the altar on the left.

A wedding dress in the style of Princess Beatrice's, who married in the church.

The princess and her husband are buried here. In the churchyard are the graves of many people who worked in Osborne House in the 1800s.

CHAPTER 15

SANDOWN AND SANDOWN PIER
PIER STREET, SANDOWN PO36 8JP

Sandown is situated in the Southeast of the Island, and is great for a rainy day as well as a sunny one. If the weather is good then you can relax on the sandy beach which stretches for miles, but if it's not so wonderful there are a few indoor places you can go to as well. The pier has plenty of amusements, rides, cafes and a bar, there are shops up the hill from the pier, and further down the coast road there is Dinosaur World, which is interesting for adults as well as children. You can stay at the Ocean Hotel, which is right on the beach, or in one of the many bed and breakfast places available. There are plenty of seafront cafes to dine in, and Sandown takes part in the carnival season every year along with many other Isle of Wight towns.

We usually eat at DeVilles along the seafront if we go to Sandown, which provides good plain food and also a bed and breakfast service.

CHAPTER 16

SHANKLIN CHINE
3 CHINE HILL, SHANKLIN, PO37 6BW

We've been visiting the Chine for many years. Shanklin Chine was the Island's first tourist attraction, and opened back in Victorian times. It consists of a ravine with paths along waterfalls, trees, and lush plants and vegetation. At night during the summer the paths are illuminated. There are sometimes exhibitions in the gift shop building, and there is a café and toilets. Here's me in my 'special seat' at the top of the Chine, which overlooks the beach.

At the top end of the Chine you can walk down to the beach with its many cafes and amusements. The other end of the Chine begins in the old town of Shanklin, where you can browse around the shops or visit a restaurant or bar. The entrance fee is not too expensive, and it's good value for money. It doesn't close until 10pm.

Along the beachfront at Shanklin is one of our favourite restaurants – The Steamer Inn. Portions are very generous, and you can sit outside if it's a nice day.

Below are some more views of the Chine, which never seems to change no matter how many years go by!

CHAPTER 17

STEEPHILL COVE
LOVE LANE, VENTNOR, PO38 1AF

We had been coming to the Island for years, before we discovered Steephill Cove. There is no direct access by car, and you have to park the car in Ventnor's Botanic Gardens car park. As the name suggests, there's a bit of a steep climb down the many steps to the beach, which was very busy when we went in the height of summer.

It's a small mainly stony beach, with quite a few cafés and bars. There's also some private apartments if you want to stay there. The best thing about it is there's no cars!

CHAPTER 18

THE ISLE OF WIGHT FESTIVAL
SEACLOSE PARK, FAIRLEE ROAD, NEWPORT, PO30 2QS

We've been attending this music festival for many years. The festival is usually the second weekend in June every year, but sometimes this can vary. Big name bands get to play here, and the festival runs from the Thursday afternoon through to the Sunday evening, finishing with fireworks after the headline band's set. There's lots to see and do at the festival, and sometimes the Red Arrows fly over too. A lot of walking is involved, so make sure you've got good legs! There are rides for the thrill seekers, stalls selling clothing and all sorts, satellite stages and a Big Top for the lesser known bands, as well as a main stage, food outlets and lots of bars. I'll share some pictures below.

CHAPTER 19

THE TENNYSON TRAIL, FRESHWATER
SATNAV APPROXIMATELY PO39 OJH

What a joy it is to still be able to walk along the cliffs to the Tennyson monument at my age of 61! With the sun on my face and not much breeze it's lovely up on Tennyson Down at Freshwater. It's a ramblers' paradise, and many walkers are usually up there with us. There's a toilet at the start of the trail, but none up on the cliffs. Once you reach the monument after 2 miles, you can either go back or carry on walking into Alum Bay. Afterwards if you still have some energy, you can visit Tennyson's home, Farringford House, also shown below.

CHAPTER 20

WINKLE STREET, CALBOURNE,
PO30 4JF

An 'olde worlde' street with picture-postcard thatched cottages just off the main road towards Freshwater. You cannot park the car there, but there are usually spaces around the corner near the church. Great for a quick visit when you're going to Alum Bay. No facilities.

CHAPTER 21

YAR ESTUARY

If you drive over to Freshwater, take the little road past the Red Lion public house (postcode PO40 9BP) and veer towards the right of the church you'll come to the Yar Estuary. There you'll see a gravel path running along the side of the estuary. This was once the Victorian Freshwater to Yarmouth railway line (closed in the 1950s), and it has now been transformed into a peaceful walkway /cycling route.

We've spent many a happy hour cycling along the few miles of disused railway. Just at the right moment a café and toilets appear on the left. The café building was once the station house and ticket office, and a few of the old train seats have been installed inside the café.

Outside the café ducks waddle about near a stream. You can buy duck food at the café for £1 (there are notices about not to give them bread).

A lovely morning or afternoon out with your hiking partner or cycling companion! The old station master's house can be seen in the distance in the photo below, which marks the start of the walkway. We were once shown around the house by its very hospitable owner. The property has been extended now, but just two rooms once housed the Victorian station master, his wife, and their 11 children!

WEBSITE LINKS OF OTHER PLACES TO VISIT

We might not have been to these places, but they all seem like great places to visit with the family:

Blackgang Chine:
https://blackgangchine.com/

Tapnell Farm Park:
https://www.tapnellfarmpark.com/

Isle Jump:
https://www.islejump.co.uk/

Isle of Wight Pearl:
https://iowpearl.com/

Yarmouth Castle:
https://www.english-heritage.org.uk/visit/places/yarmouth-castle/

RECOMMENDED RESTAURANTS:

The Steamer Inn, Shanklin

The Yarbridge Inn, Sandown

The Crab & Lobster, Bembridge

The Appley Manor Hotel, Ryde

Note to Readers:
Please email me at **Glenda.shepherd@btconnect.com** with any other recommendations so that I can add them to this list.

www.ingramcontent.com/pod-product-compliance
Lightning Source LLC
Chambersburg PA
CBHW052116070526
44584CB00017B/2509